ELEPHANTS!
Strange and Wonderful

Laurence Pringle

Illustrated by
Meryl Henderson

BOYDS MILLS PRESS
AN IMPRINT OF BOYDS MILLS & KANE
New York

For Carola and Ellis Chase, steadfast friends for more than four decades,
and reliable sources of love, laughter, and good food.
—LP

In memory of my brother, Ralph, who knew how to live life to the fullest!
He will be missed.
—MH

The author and illustrator would like to thank Cynthia Moss,
director of the Amboseli Trust for Elephants, and the
longest-running elephant research project in the world,
for her careful review of the text and illustrations.

Text copyright © 2021 by Laurence Pringle
Illustrations copyright © 2021 by Meryl Henderson

For information about permission to reproduce selections from this book,
please contact permissions@bmkbooks.com.

Boyds Mills Press
An imprint of Boyds Mills & Kane, a division of Astra Publishing House
boydsmillspress.com

Printed in China
ISBN: 978-1-63592-479-4 (hc)
ISBN: 978-1-63592-472-5 (eBook)
Library of Congress Control Number: 2020947703

First edition
10 9 8 7 6 5 4 3 2 1

The text is set in Goudy Old Style.
The illustrations are done in watercolor and pencil.

Just for a moment, close your eyes and imagine that you are an elephant.

Wow! If you ever wanted to be taller, now you are. You tower over those humans down there.

Now feel your big ears. They cover your shoulders! You can move them a lot, and even flap them in the air to cool yourself on a hot day.

Best of all is your amazing nose. It is a muscular trunk, long enough to reach your toes. Use it to squirt water, lift logs, or grab fruit from trees high overhead!

You can even use the tip of your nose-trunk to turn the page and learn more about extraordinary elephants.

Back *is rounded, bulging upward*

Ears *are big, but less than half the size of African savanna elephants*

Forehead, *seen from the front, has a double dome*

Asian elephants are smaller than African savanna elephants, but they are still very big. A male Asian elephant, called a bull, can grow to be nine feet tall and weigh 9,500 pounds. Its body can measure twenty-six feet long. Asian elephants live in Southern and Southeast Asia, including India, Cambodia, Thailand, and Malaysia.

Tusks *grow in most Asian males, not in females*

Trunk *has a tip with one lobe, or finger*

For many years people believed that there were two kinds, or species, of elephants—one in Asia, one in Africa. Scientists knew that populations of African elephants differed in some ways, but still believed they were all one species. Then, in 2010, came surprising news. New evidence from the study of **genetics** revealed that African elephants were two separate species.

One African species lives mostly in open savanna habitat—grassland studded with bushes and trees. This species is called the **savanna**, or bush, elephant. The other, the forest elephant, lives mostly in dense forests. These two African species, along with the one Asian species, are shown on these pages.

Ears *are the biggest of all animals*

Forehead, *seen from the front, has a single dome*

Back *is flat or bows downward*

Trunk *has two lobes, or fingers, on the tip*

Tusks *are long, curved, and light-colored*

African savanna elephants are the biggest of all land animals. A bull can grow to be twelve feet tall and thirty feet long. It can weigh as much as 15,000 pounds. A female (cow) is smaller but can still weigh up to 7,000 pounds. The savanna species lives in eastern and southern Africa and parts of western Africa.

Ears *are about half the size of the savanna elephant's ears*

Forehead, *seen from the front, has a single dome*

Back *is flat or bows downward*

Skin *color is darkest of all elephants*

Tusks *are brown and point downward*

African forest elephants are the smallest of the three species. They weigh about half as much as savanna elephants and live in the rainforests of central and western Africa.

Trunk *has two lobes, or fingers, on the tip*

5

An elephant's nose is called a **trunk**. From study of ancient bones, teeth, and other **fossils**, scientists know that other big **mammals** with long trunks lived long ago. Another name for a long trunk is a **proboscis**, so scientists call the group of big, long-nosed mammals **Proboscidea**. Fossil remains of extinct kinds reveal that many of them also had tusks, as today's elephants do.

The best known of these long-dead proboscideans are mammoths and mastodons. They are shown here with others that lived millions of years long ago.

The tusks of Deinotherium were in its lower jaw and curved downward. They may have been used for digging roots or whole plants out of the ground. Deinotherium lived for about 25 million years, and became extinct about a million years ago.

Gomphotheres also lived for a span of many millions of years. They had long jaws, with tusks on both top and bottom. Gomphotheres fossils have been found in Europe, China, Africa, and North America.

Stegodon had huge tusks that grew close together. Its trunk probably moved around above the tusks, not between them like an elephant's trunk does. Fossils found on an island in Indonesia show that a population of dwarf Stegodons lived there until about 12,000 years ago.

Mastodons lived on many continents, including both North and South America. They were covered with reddish-brown hair, and their legs were shorter than those of today's elephants. Mastodons were probably forest dwellers. From the shape of their teeth, scientists believe they fed on tough twigs and leaves of trees and shrubs, not soft grasses.

Mammoths had long coats, and the best-known species is called the woolly mammoth. The tusks of male mammoths grew to as long as fourteen feet. Bones and other fossils of mammoths have been discovered in China, Mexico, and the Arctic. They have also been unearthed in a Michigan soybean field, and under part of an Oregon college football field!

Most remarkable are remains of mammoths that died in the Arctic just a few thousand years ago. Whole mammoth bodies have been found in frozen earth (**permafrost**). Freezing temperatures kept soft parts from decaying. Today, scientists are able to study hair, muscles, and even partly digested food that a mammoth ate just before it died.

Considering the long history of life on Earth, mammoths died out "recently." The last mammoth passed away about 4,000 years ago on a Siberian island.

Elephants are by far the biggest of all land animals. They loom large in nature, and also in human imaginations. Throughout history, elephants have inspired myths and legends. They are symbols of power and wisdom. In ancient cultures elephants were believed to be gods, or were at least linked closely to gods. For thousands of years they have inspired artists, beginning with those who painted images of mammoths, mastodons, and elephants on cave walls. In more recent times, elephant characters in children's stories are usually heroes, powerful but also gentle and friendly. Think of Babar, created by Jean de Brunhoff, or of *Horton Hears a Who* by Dr. Seuss.

In Africa and Europe, people painted and carved images of animals that were important in their lives. In South Africa, paintings from many thousands of years ago show elephants, sometimes with humans.

Elephant folktales tell how they got their trunks—and also how they lost their wings! According to a story from India, the first elephants could fly. One day an elephant landed in a great banyan tree. Its weight broke a branch that fell onto a teacher who was resting beneath the tree. The elephant flew to another branch. That branch broke too, causing more harm below. The teacher punished all elephants, taking their wings away forever. (Imagine, a teacher with such powers!)

Ganesha, a Hindu god, has the head and trunk of an elephant. Images of Ganesha—statues, paintings, and jewelry—are common throughout India, Nepal, and Sri Lanka. Ganesha is the god of education, knowledge, wisdom, and wealth. He is thought to bring joy and good luck to people in business, to travelers, and to students. On the other hand, Ganesha can put obstacles in the way of evildoers.

People believe that, for best results, a Ganesha statue should be placed at the front door. Different parts of Ganesha offer wisdom and advice—for example, large ears are a symbol for "Listen more," and a small mouth means "Talk less."

The trunk of an African elephant has two fingerlike lobes. It picks up objects by squeezing them between these lobes, the way you grip things between your thumb and a finger.

The trunk of an Asian elephant has just one fingerlike lobe at its tip. The elephant picks up small objects by gripping them between its lobe and the opposite edge of its nose.

For a drink, an elephant sucks a gallon or two of water into the nostrils at the tip of its trunk. Then it puts the tip of its trunk into its mouth, tilts its head back, and squirts the water down its throat. To bathe or to cool off on hot days, it can spray water over its back and shoulders.

Underwater, an elephant can raise its trunk into the air and still breathe through its nostrils. This can be vital for a small elephant crossing a river.

There is probably no animal part more useful than an elephant's trunk. It serves as a fifth limb, and a hand. First, of course, it is a nose . . . but no ordinary nose. Like your nose, a trunk has two nostrils. However, an elephant's nose is very long. The nostril tubes inside its trunk can be as long as eight feet. Trunks take in and let out air, and detect odors—from the ground below or a dozen miles away.

A trunk is actually part upper lip, part nose. It has no bones, but it does have more than 40,000 muscles. It can flex, curl, and stretch. It can suck up water and then spray or squirt it out. It can dig and pull and lift all sorts of objects, and also hug another elephant. And an elephant can use the tip on its trunk to wipe away dirt from its eye, scratch behind its ear, or pick up a nut from the ground.

11

The trunks of elephants are remarkable, but so are their feet, teeth, ears, and skin.

The skin on an elephant's head or back can be as much as an inch thick. (An elephant is sometimes called a **pachyderm** because that word, in Greek, means "thick-skinned.") The skin is very wrinkly. Wrinkles hold water, and that helps elephants keep cool in the hot climates where they live.

The great weight of an elephant is supported by its stout, round legs, with large leg bones within. The bottoms of its feet spread wide when it steps on the ground, then get smaller when lifted. Elephants walk on their tiptoes and support their weight mostly on pads of dense fat in their heels. Despite their size, they can move very quietly. (They can also walk backward very well.) The thick soles on the bottoms of their feet have patterns of cracks and grooves, like the tread on athletic shoes. This helps elephants grip the ground and avoid slipping.

Elephant ears act as air conditioners in two different ways. Flapping them back and forth fans air over the elephant's skin. (It also chases away annoying flies.) More important, ear flapping actually cools the elephant's blood. The ears have thin skin and contain many blood vessels close to the surface. An elephant's ear flapping causes air to pass over that surface and carry heat away. The blood is then cooler as it flows to other parts of the body.

Elephant eyes are small for such a big animal, but their eyelashes can grow to be five inches long.

Many mammals, including humans, have cutting teeth called **incisors**. You have eight—the four front teeth in your upper and lower jaws. Elephants have just two incisors in their upper jaws. These grow into **tusks** that grow throughout an elephant's life. Tusks can be several feet long and weigh more than 200 pounds. They can be weapons, or shovels (digging for water or plant food), or chisels (peeling bark for food from trees). Also, an elephant can "pick its nose" with the tip of a tusk.

Molars are teeth suited to grinding up food. Elephants have just four, but they are huge, up to a foot long! Molars grind up tough plant parts, so they wear down. Worn-down molars are gradually replaced by new and bigger ones. In its lifetime, an elephant has six sets of these vital teeth.

Earth's biggest land animals also have gigantic appetites. Wild adult elephants eat as much as 400 pounds of plant food a day. They spend sixteen or more hours every day and night looking for food, eating, and drinking water. Their food is only partly digested, so elephants sometimes produce 300 pounds of **dung** (also called manure, or poop) in a day. Wherever they roam, their dung helps make the soil more fertile. It often contains plant seeds. Some of the seeds are food for birds, insects, and other animals. Some may sprout and grow to be trees.

An elephant eats plants of many kinds, and their parts: leaves, roots, twigs, branches, bark, bushes, grasses, seeds, flowers, and fruit. The elephant's diet varies with changing seasons, and with different **habitats**.

In their rainforest habitat, African forest elephants eat many kinds of fruit. African savanna elephants live in more open, grassy habitat. They eat well during rainy times, when there is a lush growth of grasses. They grab bunches of grasses with their trunks, knock soil off the roots, then stuff the grasses into their mouths and chomp with their molars. In the dry season, grasses are usually scarce. Elephants then seek leaves, bark, and other woody food. They may walk thirty miles a day to find enough to eat.

Because they live in hot African and Asian climates, water is precious for elephants—for drinking, of course, but also for bathing and for play. An adult elephant can drink between thirty and fifty gallons a day. That's a lot, and in dry seasons or under drought conditions, elephants may have to make do with less.

They try to stay close to a good water supply. Sometimes they have to dig for water. With tusks and feet they dig in a dry riverbed, or at a dried-up water hole, to reach water below the surface. The water they unearth is vital for them and also for many other animals.

Elephants dig to reach water, and also to find soil and rocks that contain salt and minerals they need in their diet but don't get from plants they eat.

Young or old, elephants like to frolic and roll in water, and in mud. A coating of mud has a cooling effect. It protects elephant skin from sun and heat. Elephants sometimes snort dusty soil into their trunks, then spray it over their bodies. These dust baths can also help keep them a bit cooler.

17

Elephant families are usually led by a big, old, wise female: a **matriarch**. In their long lives, matriarchs learn and remember a lot. They know where to find food and water—every day and also in different seasons. They know the best routes to take as they lead their families on long migrations. In Africa's Namibian desert, elephant families often travel many hundreds of miles and visit some drinking pools only once in a year. Matriarchs remember, and know where to go.

An elephant family may include four generations, from newborn calves to a matriarch great-grandmother as old as sixty years. The calves are both females and males. The females stay with their family for their whole lives. By the time a female calf is five years old, she starts being a helpful babysitter for younger ones. (An older female that helps care for calves is called an **allomother**.) Males leave the family when they reach their teen years. These teenagers may wander alone, or form groups with other bulls. They learn from older bulls, but old or young, bull elephants are drifters. They are not as closely bonded as the mostly female families led by matriarchs, but they do form friendships with other bulls.

Members of an elephant family have strong bonds. They care about, and watch out for, one another. A matriarch tries to keep her family safe. When lions threaten a calf, she and the older females often form a protective circle around their young. Scientists who study elephants call this behavior **bunching**.

19

Elephants form close social bonds, and keep in touch in several ways. They touch a lot, with their trunks, bodies, feet, and tails. Near and far, they send and receive lots of information.

Using their keen sense of smell, elephants learn about one another by sniffing faces and bodies. They also learn by watching "body language." Elephants have many ways of "talking," by moving their ears, trunks, legs, tails, and bodies. The motions of elephant ears and heads can alert others to danger, make threats, or express friendliness. A head wiggle is a play signal.

People usually know two elephant sounds: loud trumpeting and low, thundery rumbles. The full range of elephant sounds is much greater and more complex. For example, there are "attack" rumbles, "let's get moving" rumbles, "let's gather together" rumbles, and at least twenty others. Elephants also scream, snort, bellow, and hum. All these sounds have meaning to elephants.

Humans can only hear parts of elephant calls. For example, we hear the upper, higher-pitched parts of elephant rumbles, but not the low-pitched parts. These **infrasounds** are below the range of human hearing. Elephants can probably hear infrasounds from other elephants as far as six miles away.

Elephants also communicate by **seismic signals**—vibrations that travel through the ground. Loud rumbles can produce seismic vibrations. Elephants have special cells in their feet and in their trunks that are sensitive to seismic signals. An elephant stamping its foot can be felt and understood by other elephants, even if they are miles away.

Since elephant families travel long distances and are often far apart, seismic and infrasound signals help them communicate.

One event that causes elephants to dance and sing—in elephant ways—is the birth of a calf. Family members rumble, trumpet, and scream. Females of the family may drop to their knees, hold their heads high, and swing their trunks wildly. They touch and smell the mother and the calf. Fluids from their **temporal glands** run down their cheeks. The elephants are not crying, but they sure are excited.

Within an hour, with help from its mother and often from other females, the calf learns to stand on its wobbly legs. Soon it has its first meal of milk from one of two breasts that are between its mother's front legs. The calf hasn't learned to use its trunk for drinking. Instead, it sucks milk with its mouth.

Elephants reproduce slowly, so each calf is precious. While a mouse may have twenty young in its first year, a female elephant is often eleven years old before she is ready to mate. Then about twenty-two months pass as a calf develops within her. This **gestation period** is the longest of all mammals. (In humans, it is nine months.)

An elephant calf also needs a lot of parental care. It has so much to learn! For example, a calf needs about three years just to learn how to drink with its trunk. So it is good for a calf, and the well-being of the whole family, that cows give birth only every four to six years.

Young males are capable of mating in their teens, but they don't get the chance because they are not as big and strong as the older bulls that elephant cows prefer. Males grow throughout their lives, so a teenager is much smaller than a big male in his forties.

One sign that a bull is ready to mate is fluid running down its cheeks from its temporal glands. This warns that a bull has reached a temporary condition called **musth**. A bull can be in musth for three months of each year. Bulls in musth can be unpredictable. They are aggressive toward other bulls—and sometimes toward people.

All through their lives, elephants show how they care about others in their family. They do it with day-to-day touches and sounds. They do it by teaching calves which plants are good to eat. And they do it in emergency situations.

If a calf is stuck in mud, or having trouble crossing a river, adults do their best to rescue it. If an elephant is injured and can't walk at a normal pace, its whole family slows down. An elephant's death is especially troubling to the members of its family. They may try for hours to lift a dead companion to its feet.

An elephant that lives its whole natural life can reach about sixty-five years of age. Then it may die for a simple reason: its sixth and very last set of molar teeth are worn down. These teeth come into use at about age forty-three. Eventually they wear out. An old elephant can get food but not chew it. The elephant grows weaker and often starves to death.

Sometimes a family finds the bones of a long-dead elephant. The elephants smell, fondle, and even pick up the bones and tusks. Scientists wonder: what are they learning? Do the elephants recognize an individual they once knew?

More than three thousand years ago, people began to capture, tame, and train elephants to do work. All three species of elephants have been tamed and used for many tasks. Today tourists can enjoy elephant-back rides, but long ago elephants carried warriors into battle.

War elephants were used in conflicts between ancient kingdoms in Asia. A famous military use happened more than 2,300 years ago. The army of Hannibal of Carthage (an ancient city in North Africa) included nearly forty African elephants. Hannibal hoped that elephants would help him conquer the Roman Empire.

His army crossed Spain, southern France, and the Alps. However, before any battles in Italy, cold weather and lack of food caused nearly all of the elephants to die.

For many centuries, and continuing today, elephants are used to haul things. The power of Asian elephants, especially, is used to carry and pull logs cut down in forests. In India, highly decorated elephants often appear at wedding receptions, parades, and other important events.

Since elephants are among the smartest of all animals, they can be trained to perform all sorts of tricks. They have long been circus stars. However, they are still elephants—animals that normally have rich social lives and close ties with others of their kind. Many people believe that it is cruel to keep elephants in circuses. Change is happening. Fewer circuses have them. In the United States, the Ringling Bros. and Barnum & Bailey Circus, which had featured elephant acts, went out of business in 2017.

A few centuries ago, millions of elephants lived in wild habitats from China to Africa. As recently as 1900, there were 10 million elephants on Earth.

All that has changed. By 2018, only about 400,000 elephants survived in Africa. In Asia, about 40,000 remained. One reason for this dramatic change is loss of habitat. As human numbers grow, farms and villages replace wild lands where elephants once lived. Elephant families still try to follow old routes to places where they fed before. They can be a threat to both crops and people. Many elephants are killed by people protecting their property. Efforts are being made to solve these problems, but meanwhile people develop more land. More elephant habitat disappears.

Millions of elephants have also been killed for just one part of their bodies: their tusks. These giant teeth are made of **ivory**. For thousands of years this gleaming white material has been carved into statues, jewelry, chopsticks, and many other objects. The value of ivory rises as elephants grow more scarce. To stop the loss of elephants, some African and Asian nations limit or forbid hunting. However, laws have not stopped illegal, heavily armed **poachers**. Each year they kill many thousands of elephants. They also kill rangers who try to protect elephants in national parks and other elephant reserves.

Big tusks bring the most money, so the oldest, biggest elephants are often the first killed. Many matriarchs die. This is a terrible blow to elephant families. When a wise old leader dies, so does decades of knowledge stored in her memory. Scientists report that some surviving elephant families have no old adult leaders. They are made up only of young orphans.

No doubt, elephants are in big trouble. The African forest species, in particular, may be in danger of extinction. Also, poachers sometimes kill elephants to sell for meat, not just tusks. This means that any wild elephant, even a calf, may not be safe in some areas.

The situation is grim, but not hopeless. Many people, conservation groups, and nations are working to save elephants. Part of this effort is aimed at stopping poachers. More important are steps taken to stop people from buying items made of ivory. If buying stops, killing can too.

A vital action needed to save elephants is to teach or remind people of where ivory comes from. A piece of jewelry, or anything made of ivory, is part of a once-living elephant. It came from a big, intelligent, long-lived mammal. Conservation groups aim to convince people all over the world, "Don't Buy Ivory!"

The United States banned almost all trade of elephant ivory in 2016. Soon after, there was hopeful news from China. More than half the ivory sales in the world are in China, where ivory carving and selling is a big business. Beginning in 2012, people trying to save elephants paid for a Say No to Ivory advertising campaign in China. Then, in 2017, the Chinese government vowed to shut down all stages of the ivory trade by the end of that year.

This could be a turning point in the effort to save elephant populations. Of course, the ban in China will only succeed if it is enforced. Smuggling of ivory and illegal sales of ivory must be stopped too.

If enough people change their ideas about ivory, and about the value of wild elephants, these amazing animals can be saved. In their own way, elephants are smart and strong, but now their survival depends entirely on humans. People will need to work hard to ensure that elephants can live and thrive in their wild habitats.

Glossary

allomother—A female elephant that helps take care of the young of other members of its family.

bunching—Elephant behavior in which older females form a defensive line or circle to protect themselves and especially the young of their family.

dung—Solid body waste of animals, also called droppings, manure, or poop.

fossils—Bones, teeth, footprints, leaf imprints, and other traces of animals or plants from past ages that are preserved, usually in rocks.

Ganesha—A Hindu god who is part human, part elephant.

genetics—The study of the heredity of living things, or how characteristics of one generation are passed to generations that follow.

gestation period—The length of time from when an animal first starts to develop within its mother until it is born. Elephant gestation time, about twenty-two months, is the longest of all. Next longest: sperm whale, about eighteen months.

habitat—The place or environment where an organism normally lives.

incisors—Front teeth in the upper and lower jaws of many mammals. In elephants, two upper-jaw incisors grow to be tusks.

infrasounds—Very low sounds that are below the hearing range of humans.

ivory—A hard white substance, the major part of elephant tusks, which has been carved into jewelry and many other objects. Material similar to ivory also makes up the teeth of sperm whales, walruses, and hippos.

mammals—Warm-blooded animals with hair whose young are fed milk from their mother's mammary glands.

matriarch—A wise old female leader of an elephant family.

molars—Teeth with broad chewing surfaces that grind up food.

musth—In bull elephants, a time of readiness to mate with cows and also to be aggressive toward other bulls.

pachyderm—In Greek, a word meaning "thick skin." Elephants, hippopotamuses, and rhinoceroses are sometimes called pachyderms. All have unusually thick skin on much of their bodies.

permafrost—Earth that is usually frozen year-round, and often for thousands of years.

poachers—People who hunt or fish illegally.

Proboscidea—The scientific name of a kind of large-bodied mammals with large tusks and long trunks. Elephants are the only living proboscideans. Many other species, including mammoths, died out long ago.

proboscis—A nose, especially the long, flexible nose-trunk of elephants.

savanna—A habitat of open grassland with scattered trees and shrubs.

seismic signals—Ground vibrations that elephants can detect with their feet and trunks.

temporal glands—Glands located at the temples of elephants' heads (between the eyes and the ears) that produce strong-smelling fluids that send information to other elephants.

trunk—A unique kind of "limb" formed of an elephant's upper lip and nose. Strong and flexible, it can be used to breathe, smell, and drink, and also to get food, play, and fight.

tusks—An elephant's long incisor teeth that grow from the front of its upper jaw.

To Learn More

Books and Periodicals

Buzzeo, Toni. *A Passion for Elephants: The Real Life Adventure of Field Scientist Cynthia Moss*. New York: Dial, 2015.

Joubert, Beverly and Dereck. *Face to Face with Elephants*. Washington, DC: National Geographic, 2008.

Moss, Cynthia. *Little Big Ears: The Story of Ely*. New York: Simon & Schuster, 1996.

Mueller, Tom. "Ice Baby." *National Geographic*, May 2009, pp. 30–55.

Newman, Patricia. *Eavesdropping on Elephants*. Minneapolis: Lerner, 2019.

O'Connell, Caitlin and Donna M. Jackson. *The Elephant Scientist*. Boston: Houghton Mifflin Harcourt, 2011.

Pringle, Laurence. *Elephant Woman: Exploring the World of Elephants*. New York: Atheneum, 1997.

Websites*

elephantconservation.org
International Elephant Foundation

elephantsforafrica.org
Elephants for Africa

elephanttrust.org
Amboseli Trust for Elephants

savetheelephants.org
Save the Elephants

worldwildlife.org
World Wildlife Fund

*active at time of publication

Sources

Main sources of information include the following books and periodicals, some written by elephant researchers.

Alter, Stephen. *Elephas Maximus: A Portrait of the Indian Elephant*. New York: Harcourt, 2004.

Christ, Bryan. "Tracking Ivory." *National Geographic*, September 2015, pages 32–59.

Moss, Cynthia. *Elephant Memories: Thirteen Years in the Life of an Elephant Family*. New York: William Morrow, 1988.

O'Connell, Caitlin. *The Elephant's Secret Sense*: *The Hidden Life of the Wild Herds in Africa*. New York: Free Press, 2007.

Peterson, Dale. *Elephant Reflections*. Berkeley, CA: University of California Press, 2009.

Poole, Joyce. *Elephants*. Stillwater, MN: Voyageur Press, 1997.

Poole, Joyce. *Coming of Age with Elephants*. New York: Hyperion, 1996.

Yee, Amy. "Following in Huge Footsteps." *New York Times*, July 5, 2016, pages D1, D3.

Index